SPEAKING FROM THE HEART

18 LANGUAGES FOR MODERN LOVE

ANNE HODDER-SHIPP, CSE

COPYRIGHT © 2024 ANNE HODDER-SHIPP

PUBLISHED BY SHOEBOX PRESS
3439 NE SANDY BLVD. #705
PORTLAND, OR 97232

All rights reserved. This book may not be reproduced in whole or in part without written permission from the author; nor may any part of this book be reproduced, stored in any retrieval system, or transmitted in any form or by any means other than by book or ebook purchase, unless otherwise permitted by the author.

COVER ILLUSTRATION & DESIGN VIA CANVA.COM
© 2021 CANVA.COM

INTERIOR ILLUSTRATIONS VIA CANVA.COM
© 2021 CANVA.COM

ALL RIGHTS RESERVED. STOCK MEDIA USED WITH PERMISSION SUBJECT TO FREE IMAGES LICENSE TERMS.

ISBN 978-1-7369049-6-1

PRAISE FOR
SPEAKING FROM THE HEART:
18 LANGUAGES FOR MODERN LOVE

"Anne Hodder-Shipp's *Speaking from the Heart: 18 Languages for Modern Love* is the [alternative] to *The 5 Love Languages®* society has needed for decades. It is a refreshing and inclusive look at the ways we connect in relationships and will help clinicians, coaches, sex educators, and anyone attempting to engage in relationships with other humans as we navigate the messiness of life. I look forward to utilizing this ebook with my clients as a means of aiding their relational growth and highly recommend it to everyone!"

KRISTINE IVES, LMFT, CET-2 (SHE/HER) CERTIFIED BRAINSPOTTING THERAPIST & CO-FOUNDER OF BRAVEHEART RETREATS

"*Speaking from the Heart: 18 Languages for Modern Love* has been my fave book purchase/read this year!!"!

A KIND READER FROM INSTAGRAM :)

"This is a brilliant foundational guide for people of all ages and identities who are ready to level up their relationship skills. Practical, relevant, and user-friendly, *Speaking from the Heart* offers dozens of specific examples for how to match your feelings of love with actionable, identifiable behaviors that build connection and nourish humanity in the 21st century. No longer left wondering, "How do I show them I care?", *Speaking from the Heart* guides you to understand how and why love matters in your world. For friends and lovers, coworkers and neighbors, *Speaking from the Heart* shows you how to build community and connections that thrive, one relationship at a time."

CYNDI DARNELL (SHE/HER,
SEX & RELATIONSHIP THERAPIST

"With *Speaking from the Heart: 18 Languages for Modern Love*, Anne Hodder-Shipp has taken the love language 'software' and conceived a contemporary and more inclusive paradigm with which to navigate and nourish relationships. With compassion, clarity, and wit, Anne has created an expansive lexicon of love for the 21st century."

ELLE CHASE, CSE (SHE/HER)
CERTIFIED SEX EDUCATOR & BODY
ACCEPTANCE COACH

"This book is a fantastically accessible read. As a Disability Awareness Consultant working in sexuality and disability, I had heard of *The 5 Love Languages®*, but I never honestly understood them or thought that they could be applicable to me in any way. *Speaking from the Heart: 18 Languages for Modern Love* helped me to see what my love languages are and some of the ways that I have used them incorrectly. This ebook will act as a comprehensive guide for someone understanding love languages for the very first time, but will also be a welcome and necessary refresher for those who felt that *The 5 Love Languages®* didn't fully encompass their experiences. My favorite part of this ebook is the knowledge Anne brings to the complexity and nuance found in all types of relationships, and I think that is what sets this updated version far apart from the original."

ANDREW GURZA (THEY/HE)
DISABILITY AWARENESS CONSULTANT &
HOST OF "DISABILITY AFTER DARK"
PODCAST

"This is such a HUGE gift to the world!"

ANOTHER KIND READER FROM INSTAGRAM :)

"*Speaking from the Heart: 18 Languages for Modern Love* is so emblematic of Anne's approach to teaching about sexuality and relationships. Above all else, *SFTH* is inclusive of all expressions of love and relationship styles, which is such an important reimagining of and alternative to *The 5 Love Languages*®. In addition to being an accessible resource, it is a fun and engaging read with practical examples that are brought to life through illustration. The way that Anne approaches love languages is expansive and full of empathy, which imbues it with a permission-giving quality. *SFTH* presents a new methodology that is sure to expand the awareness and relevance of the love language theory."

SARAH TOMCHESSON (SHE/HER)
SEX EDUCATOR, FOUNDER OF DAMIANA CONSULTING & CO-FOUNDER OF S3X PLUS

"I'm impressed, elated, and swooning over Anne's work. Thank you so much for creating a tool that I can use with my clients that isn't rooted in religious smegma."

KRISTINE D'ANGELO, CSC (SHE/HER)
CLINICAL SEXOLOGIST & SEX COACH

"As a sexuality educator with a focus in Asexuality and Aromanticism, I was absolutely thrilled to find a book that explores languages of love that centers platonic connections. Being able to explore the vastness of how we can receive and share love throughout our lives in whatever form our relationships might take is an empowering and liberating journey. Anne Hodder-Shipp breaks down these nuanced and complex concepts into accessible and expansive language that is affirming and inclusive."

AUBRI LANCASTER, BA², CSE (SHE/HER)
AASECT CERTIFIED SEX EDUCATOR

"Cuddling up with my partner to read *Speaking from the Heart: 18 Languages for Modern Love* together sparked more emotional intimacy in our relationship! We had a healing discussion about the types of love we did and didn't receive as children. My favorite part is the confidence I feel now in our shared understanding of how best to meet each other's love needs."

KAMI ORANGE (SHE/HER)
BOUNDARY COACH

"Love is inclusive. Anne's book highlights this inclusivity in their guide to relational love communication. This book is needed, and I will be recommending it to everyone I work with. Every page overflows with strategies to understand and communicate intentional love as well as disrupt harmful messages often found in cis-normative and heteronormative media and literature. We are all uniquely layered with way more than five ways to express love — this is the guide you need to inquire within yourself and others about ways of expressing and experiencing love."

DR. GRACE ABRUZZO (THEY/THEM)
CERTIFIED PELVIC HEALTH & OBSTETRIC HEALTH PHYSICAL THERAPIST

TO MY COYOTE

(BARF)

THANK YOUS & ACKNOWLEDGMENTS

Collaboration and community is a key part of my life and work. The people listed below have played important roles in my life, including helping me become a better person or professional, or supporting the success of the 18 Modern Love Languages. Please check out their work, buy their books or courses, revel in their brilliance, and tell your friends!

NATHANIEL HODDER-SHIPP
ELLE CHASE
SANDRA ANN MILLER
SARAH TOMCHESSON
DR. GRACE ABRUZZO
DR. BIANCA LAUREANO
KAMI ORANGE
KEZIA VIDA

PAULA LEECH
CYNDI DARNELL
DR. EMILY NAGOSKI
ADRIENNE MAREE BROWN
BELL HOOKS
DR. JULIA B. COLWELL
SONYA RENEE TAYLOR
ESTHER PEREL

Plus a HUGE thanks to everyone who's taken the time to post or comment about my work on social media.

Word of mouth is powerful!

TABLE OF CONTENTS

A NOTE ABOUT ATTRIBUTION	1
A NOTE ABOUT ACCESSIBILITY	2
A NOTE ABOUT THIS CONTENT	3
ANOTHER NOTE ABOUT THIS CONTENT	4
FEELINGS WHEELS	5
HELLO, DEAR READER	7
"LOVE," "RELATIONSHIP," & "PLATONIC"	12
SEXUAL ASSAULT, ABUSE, & VIOLENCE RESOURCES/HOTLINES	19-21
ANSWERS TO COMMON QUESTIONS	22
THE 18 MODERN LOVE LANGUAGES	33
ACCOUNTABILITY	35

TABLE OF CONTENTS

ACTIVE LISTENING	38
ACTS OF EMPATHY	41
AFFIRMING COMMUNICATION	44
BESTOWING	47
EMOTIONAL LABOR	50
ENGAGED EXPERIENCES	53
INTENTIONAL TIME	56
PERSONAL GROWTH	59
PLATONIC TOUCH	62
PROBLEM-SOLVING	65
PROVIDING	68

TABLE OF CONTENTS

SHARED BELIEFS	71
SOLIDARITY	74
TEAMWORK	77
THOUGHTFUL SERVICE	80
UNDIVIDED ATTENTION	83
UPSKILLING	86
SELF CHECK-IN	89
A NOTE ABOUT SELF- & CO-REGULATION	90
SPECIAL THANK-YOU	93
IMPORTANT POINTS TO LEAVE WITH	94
KEEP EXPLORING	100

TABLE OF CONTENTS

FIND ME ONLINE!	101
ABOUT THE AUTHOR	102
MORE FROM ANNE	103
SPECIAL OFFER TO READERS	104
CHEERS!	105
BLANK NOTES PAGES	106

A NOTE ABOUT ATTRIBUTION

If you feel inspired by any of the concepts, ideas, analogies, or information you read in this book and want to use them in your own workplace, community groups, professional practice, fellowship, or for someone other than yourself, I would greatly appreciate it if you would please credit me and this book, as well as any names mentioned alongside them. Maybe even provide website or social media links, too!

You do not have permission to profit from re-creating or re-printing anything you find in this book, or to pass anything you found here as your own.

You can find my formal copyright notice at the beginning of this book.

I choose to trust that you, dear reader, will do the right thing.

A NOTE ABOUT ACCESSIBILITY

It is important to acknowledge that many resources about love and relationships that are popular and available today are not as accessible as they could be. It doesn't mean they aren't effective or helpful! It does mean, though, that they don't always effectively represent the wide variety, complexity, and nuanced nature of love and how our identities and life experiences impact the way we relate to it. Love is not one-size-fits-all and cannot be taught or discussed as though it is a standard part of being human.

Many people (myself included) have felt left out or dismissed by many of these resources. My intention with the 18 Modern Love Languages is to disrupt this by discussing love and providing guidance using an expansive lens that acknowledges the wisdom and expertise that is already within each of us. A big part of my job is to simply help bring it to the surface.

A NOTE ABOUT THIS CONTENT

Speaking from the Heart: 18 Languages for Modern Love is an original work written by Anne Hodder-Shipp and published by Shoebox Press.

The author, the content of this book, and the 18 Modern Love Languages are not affiliated with *The 5 Love Languages®* series of products, Northfield Publishing, or the Moody Bible Institute.

Any reference to "love language" or "love languages" in this book is used to describe and convey the idea of the many unique and nuanced ways humans express, receive, and identify love. These references are not an implication of endorsement of *The 5 Love Languages®* or its series of books and products.

ANOTHER NOTE ABOUT THIS CONTENT

This book discusses a variety of topics related to love and relationships, which means it could be triggering or challenging for some people to read. I trust that you can care for yourself and use your own judgment about what does and doesn't feel safe to read, so please do so as you move through these pages.

This book is meant to be an accessible and easy read. Use it as a reference guide or a way to check in with yourself as you navigate your relationship with yourself and others.

If you would prefer a lengthier, more analytic approach to Languages for Modern Love, you're in luck! I'm currently writing it as you read this.

EMOTION WHEEL #1

It can be hard to name what we're feeling sometimes, so use this emotion wheel to help you find the words. The next page has another one with even more emotion words.

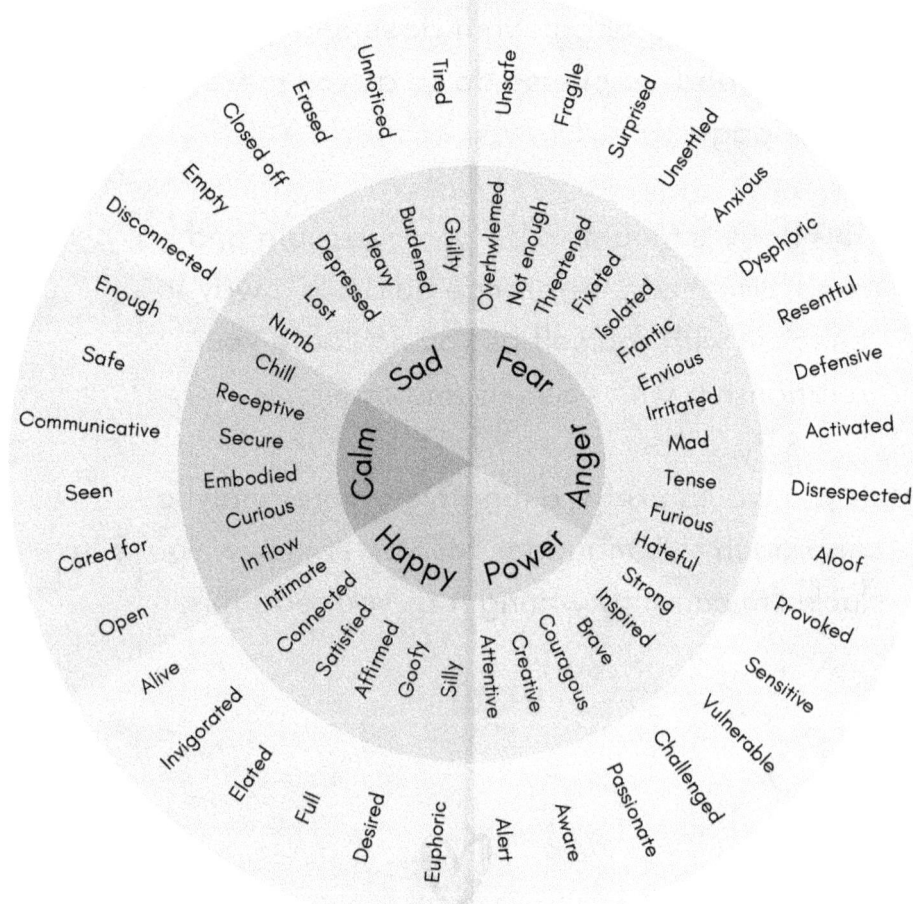

The original Feeling Wheel was created by Dr. Gloria Willcox in 1982!

EMOTION WHEEL #2

Use your two emotion wheels anytime you need help naming what you're feeling - especially while you're reading this book!

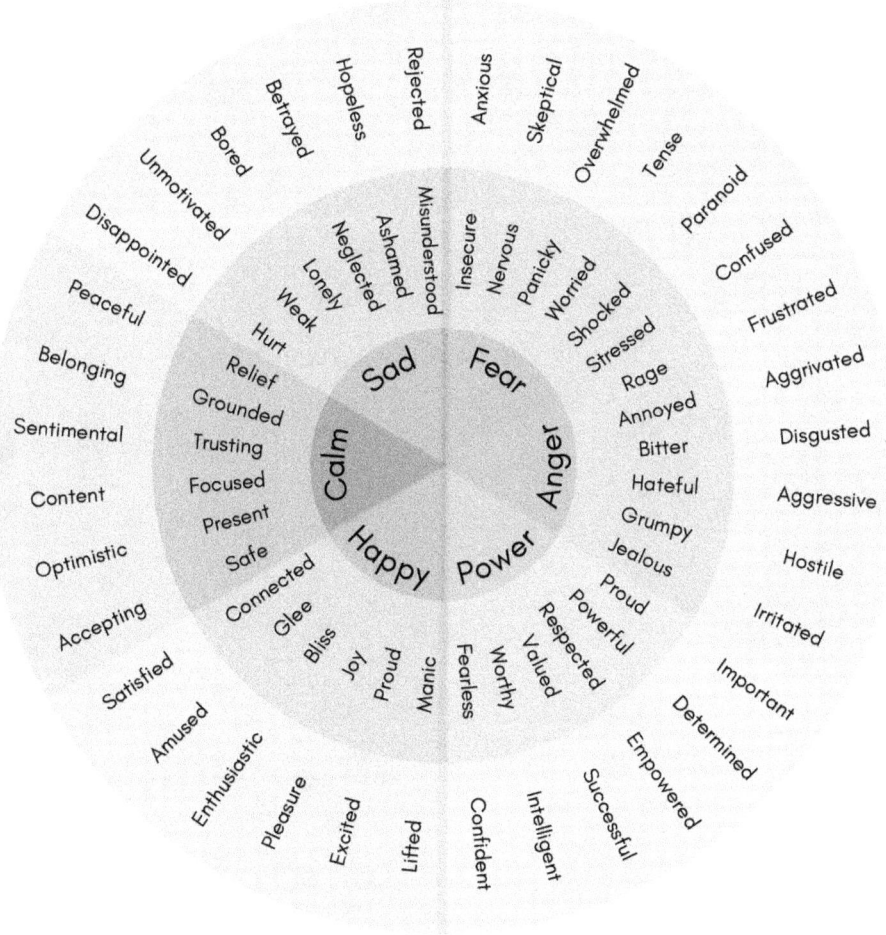

The original Feeling Wheel was created by Dr. Gloria Willcox in 1982!

HELLO, DEAR READER:

Thank you for investing in yourself (and my work!) and taking the time to get to know these valuable relational skills. While you're here, I'd love to share some of the impetus for this guide and its expanded, updated approach to the concept of love languages.

You may be familiar with love languages, an idea introduced in the early 1990s by a minister with academic roots in religious education, theology, and philosophy. The concept outlined in his popular book, *The 5 Love Languages®*, has been useful in my personal and professional work. It made love feel tangible and identifiable while acknowledging that there is more than one way to communicate it — plus it has helped countless people navigate their relationships in the hopes of figuring out what they could do differently to experience lasting love.

But there is information about this book and its author that is not openly disclosed that, were they widely known, would likely impact its international trust and acclaim. At the core is a lack of transparency that, to me personally and professionally, feels manipulative and irresponsible. I understand that what I am sharing with you is not an issue for everyone, and my goal is not to persuade you to agree with me. I simply want you to be fully informed so that you can feel and believe what feels right to you.

Though he is often described publicly as a marriage counselor, the author of *The 5 Love Languages®* holds no professional or academic training in counseling, psychology, sexuality, or relationships. He has publicly described the book's origins and that its core concept was inspired by his personal individual experiences within his own marriage and later reinforced by what he observed while giving advice to heterosexual married couples within his parish. That's it. The way he and his work have been represented has built a false sense of trust among readers and anyone who's come across *The 5 Love Languages®* and the five love languages it describes. And if that weren't enough, the author revealed his homophobia in newsletters he wrote in 2013 and 2014 meant to offer "guidance" to parents of queer kids. These writings have since been scrubbed from the internet, but the Wayback Machine Internet Archive has 'em if you want to see.

When my friends, clients, and readers learn the truth about this man, they are often shocked and dismayed, and feel lied to. Some of them become furious. I don't blame them.

There is more to know and consider about *The 5 Love Languages®* and its corresponding works. The version of *The 5 Love Languages®* currently in circulation was released in 2015 when the love language concept received a resurgence of interest thanks in part to social media. If you can get your hands on the original 1993 version, I recommend reviewing it.

The 5 Love Languages®, described by the author as "The secret to love that lasts," promotes and upholds a specific kind of relationship: heterosexual monogamous marriage. The book's content contains gendered, antiquated language; biased assumptions about romantic and sexual relationships; and emotional and behavioral expectations of men and women that are rooted in Christian theology rather than the sociology of love, gender, and identity. The book also upholds binary gender roles as though they are science and not simply constructs and rules created and enforced by dominant culture.

This does not serve – and in most cases actively harms – the people and clients in my life: transgender, non-binary, and gender-nonconforming folks; people practicing ethical non-monogamy; couples and pods with fluid sexual orientations; atheists and agnostics; asexuals and aromantics; people with ZERO interest in marriage and/or raising children; and anyone actively healing from the harm of having heteronormative gender roles and/or religious values imposed on them since birth. I wrote *Speaking from the Heart: 18 Languages for Modern Love* as an alternative to *The 5 Love Languages*® and its heteronormative, marriage-focused, romance-centered ideas that simply aren't universal to or representative of all humans and relationships. I wanted to break down the various ways that I've been able to recognize, identify, and experience love throughout my life, including its multiple fluid sources, while making space for the fact that love languages apply to ALL relationships, not just monogamous romantic bonds destined for legal recognition.

I encourage you to read through the 18 Modern Love Languages outlined in these pages and see what resonates. Notice which ones make your chest flutter or shoulders relax and which ones feel easy to just sorta skim through. Ideally, have the loved ones in your life do the same. You may learn something new or different about the way(s) you feel and express love and gain some valuable info to share with partners, friends, family members, roommates – anyone with whom you are building community and connection.

Or maybe you won't! That's OK, too. The goal is to be open to anything and everything this guide might give you. Whatever the outcome, I hope you find *Speaking from the Heart: 18 Languages for Modern Love* of some use and maybe even some solace. You deserve to ask for and receive the kinds of love that feel good for you!

BEFORE YOU DIVE IN!

I want us to get on the same page about what I have chosen to emphasize and why. This will help you navigate the 18 Modern Love Languages outlined on the next several pages.

First, the word "love." Love has a lot of meanings (and a lot of baggage) and often comes with the assumption of long-term commitment, family relation, romance, or some kind of impenetrable bond. Love is also often conflated with sex and, depending on the messaging and experiences we receive growing up, it can be tough to separate the idea of love from the act of sex. For instance, some don't feel comfortable having sex before saying the "L-word" while others actively avoid the "L-word" (also known as "catching feelings") out of fear that their friend-with-benefits (FWB) or casual sex partner will then mean something more to them.

Love is NOT something exclusively felt or experienced among family members; married spouses; long-term BFs, GFs, and partners; people practicing monogamy; twin flames or soulmates; romantic partners, or other hierarchical relationship styles. Love is universal and we can feel it toward animals, inanimate objects, political figures and celebrities, f*ck buddies, and even perfect strangers — because love is something that builds community, maintains unity, promotes compassion and empathy, acknowledges humanity, and keeps us grounded during challenging times. We don't have to earn it, buy it, or do something to be worthy of receiving it. It is not something conditional upon romance or romantic feelings, either. Love is something that helps us feel human, and it looks and feels different for everyone. For many of us, love looks and feels different depending on the relationship and can change and morph as we age, experience life, and learn more about ourselves and the world. As with pretty much any feeling, we don't really get to choose who or what we feel love toward, either, or whether we feel any love at all. This is why, for some folks, love is inconvenient, unpredictable, or something to avoid.

Love is also something that has historically been misrepresented, weaponized, and misused, leaving many people feeling that love is unsafe, harmful, or transactional. This can complicate our relationship to love as we unpack and unravel these painful experiences in order to find healing and build stronger, healthier relationships with others in our lives. It's important to acknowledge that love isn't always easy and, in many cases, it can feel downright threatening. However you feel about love, please know that I see you and your feelings are valid.

Second, the word "relationship." Relationship means different things to different people, and I find that it disproportionately is used to signify something committed, monogamous, and potentially even destined for marriage. That's not what relationship means to me. When I teach about relationship, I drill down to its most basic meaning: an interpersonal interaction. Relationships come in many forms and many of them have nothing to do with romance or planning for the future — that includes acquaintances, friends with benefits, coworkers, one-night stands Dominants/submissives, chosen family, Sugardaddies, Sugarmamas, Sugarbabies, Glucose Guardians (lol), casual encounters, caretakers/caregivers, and more.

Whether the relationship lasts two minutes or 20 years, is committed or "just casual," as long as it's consensual, it's deserving of the same level of care and respect that U.S. culture shows to marriages and long-term monogamous partnerships.

Third, the word "platonic." I make an intentional point to center the 18 Modern Love Languages around platonic, non-sexual love. As a sex educator, I want to hammer home the fact that love and sex are not synonymous. I want to help readers get familiar with the idea of love outside of the confines of traditional ideals and explore all the ways they can feel and express love — whether it's toward a best friend or the person bagging their groceries.

This is also why I refer to the language for modern love that centers physical touch as Platonic Touch. Some people believe that any kind of affectionate touch — hugging, leaning on each other, even holding hands — is sexual (or something that could lead to sex) and, as a result, declare it off limits with anyone with whom they aren't currently or planning to be physically intimate. This results in a culture of touch-starved people depending exclusively on romantic or sexual relationships in order to meet this need — often putting immense strain on those relationships. This is also a symptom of what I refer to as toxic monogamy culture, which puts excised responsibility on a romantic or sexual partner to be the sole supplier of everything a person needs to feel fulfilled. If we can learn to find and receive love from a variety of sources, we can take some of the pressure off our romantic or sexual relationships and meet our partners where they're at instead of where we'd prefer them to be.

Some people's formative lessons about love came in the context of sex, which can also make it challenging to separate loving or affectionate touch from sexual touch. I want to make it clear that the expressions of love outlined here can be present in almost any relationship, including sexual ones, but in these pages, they are intentionally presented in the context of platonic, non-sexual dynamics. And there are important reasons for this, which are outlined on the next few pages.

NOTE: The following pages contain references to consent violation, coercion, sexual abuse, and intimate partner violence, and they might be difficult to read. Feel free to skip those pages entirely!

Please take care of yourself however you need to. Many relationship resources sexualize physical touch. *The 5 Love Languages®* even refers to sex as a way to communicate its Physical Touch love language to others. While this is how many people feel about sex, it is a problematic and even harmful association. And here's why (in no particular order):

- It can frame sex as compulsory and an obligation for romantic partners to provide to each other any time it's asked for, especially within marriage.

- It can frame sex as a relationship failsafe that treats infrequent sex as the problem, rather than a symptom of the problem (if there is one), often putting the blame and responsibility on one partner.

- It can make it difficult to say "yes" to sex in a way that is given freely without any internal or external pressure.

- It can make declining sex, revoking consent, wanting to do something different, or stopping in the midst of sex challenging or even dangerous.

- It can give the false impression that one partner is entitled to the other's body as a result of their romantic and/or marital commitment.

- It can be used as a way to push, challenge, or invalidate a partner's personal and sexual boundaries.

- It can center certain sexual behaviors and turn sex into a performance of love rather than a shared experience of pleasure and play.

- It can prioritize one partner's individual desires over the other's.

- It can deprioritize or dismiss expressions of love that do not involve sexual or physical touch.

- It can pathologize lack of sexual desire, interest, or behavior as some kind of mental or emotional illness.

- It is the foundation of common sexual manipulation tactics like, "If you really loved me, you'd do this."

- It does not make space for negotiation.

- It makes having a partner decline sex feel like a personal rejection, insult, or withdrawal of love.

- It can make one partner responsible for the other's sexual desires or experiences.

If you or someone you know is experiencing intimate partner violence, sexual abuse or coercion, or needs help leaving a harmful relationship, please refer them to these resources:

- **Rape, Abuse, and Incest National Network:** https://www.rainn.org/ - 1.800.656.HOPE (4673) (24/7 hotline)

- **National Domestic Violence Hotline:** https://www.thehotline.org/get-help/ - 1.800.799.SAFE (7233) TTY 1.800.787.3224 or text "START" to 88788

- **National Coalition Against Domestic Violence:** https://ncadv.org/learn-more/resources

- **National Dating Abuse Helpline:** www.loveisrespect.org - 1.866.331.9474

- **The Trevor Project:** https://www.thetrevorproject.org/ - 1.866.488.7386 or Online Chat Support or text 678-678

Conflating sex with love is also connected to child sexual abuse, which is disproportionately committed by someone a child or their family knows personally, like a family friend or relative, neighbor, childcare provider, or teacher.

If your child or a young person in your life may be experiencing sexual abuse, please refer to these resources:

- **National Child Abuse Hotline/Childhelp:** www.childhelp.org - 1.800.4.A.CHILD (1-800-422-4453)

- **The Heal Project:** www.heal2end.org - 347.915.6115

- **Stop It Now:** www.stopitnow.org - 1.888.PREVENT (1-800-773-8368)

- **National Runaway Safeline:** www.1800runaway.org - 1.800.RUNAWAY (1-800-786-2929)

There's a lot to know about the 18 Modern Love Languages and my work. I've broken it down into questions and answers instead of a long block of text because that's how I like to learn.

What exactly is a love language?

Love languages are an idea related to the ways people express, identify, and receive love (as well as care, affection, and respect). Think about them like literal languages: there are upwards of 7,000 different languages in the world, which means there are at LEAST 7,000 different ways humans communicate with each other. Many languages also have various dialects (German has around 250!) which are like languages within a language. While we all may be saying the same or similar things, we use a wide variety of words, movements, symbols, and sounds to express them, and there is no single "official" or "correct" way to do it. Same goes for love.

Why should I learn my language(s) for modern love?

Technically, you don't have to! The 18 Modern Love Languages are one tool among many that can help build, strengthen, and maintain relationships and community. Here's why I recommend them to most of the people I work with: It can be tough (though not impossible!) to connect, understand, and relate to each other when we're speaking different languages — especially if we're expecting others to prioritize or automatically understand ours. This is why it can be helpful not only to recognize and respect all the unique ways people communicate, but to make an effort to learn about them.

Some of us have a hard time even KNOWING what we need in order to feel loved, and we may have never thought about how we show love to others. Learning about the many ways love can be expressed and received gives us options and insight. We just might end up being introduced to forms of expression that feel WAY more powerful and impactful than what we're used to.

For example, Italian might be someone's first language, but learning Afrikaans or Japanese gave them new ways to express themselves and feel heard on a different level. That doesn't mean Italian is no longer useful — it means that person has options and a deeper understanding of how they can and want to communicate with the world.

How can working with the 18 Modern Love Languages help me?

Doing this work can help us clue into the fact that the ways we've been communicating our love to others might be missing the mark, because we've been speaking Greek to folks who only understand Arabic — but blaming THEM for the miscommunication.

I'm going to take the language analogy (Anne-alogy?) even further. I believe that love is one of the most commonly misunderstood, miscommunicated, and misidentified feelings we experience in part because it's often represented as though love can only be expressed in one universal way. That would be like traveling around the world assuming that every country speaks your first language. Imagine how misunderstood, isolated, or even angry you might feel speaking Swiss German throughout Hong Kong. You might leave believing that Hongkongers are unfriendly because every time you said "Guten Morgen" they looked a little confused and replied with, "早晨." Or you might consider that, because you struggled to connect with those Hongkongers, that you're unworthy of their love, or that no one understands you. But what's ACTUALLY true? You went to Hong Kong and didn't speak a word of Cantonese!

How did you come up with the 18 Modern Love Languages?

I've always used the love language concept in my work, except with all kinds of caveats, edits, omissions, and content warnings, and, anytime I thought of an alternative or adjustment, I wrote it down. Over time, I had enough content ideas to start writing out an expanded series of more modern and nuanced love languages and, when I sat down to do it, they just poured out of me.

Why are there 18?

By the time I was done free-writing and editing, there were 18 on the page! The 18 Modern Love Languages outlined in this book are the result of 7-ish years of observation of myself and others (including hundreds of clients), and my work in the sexuality and relationships field. By no means are we limited to these 18.

I'm low-key overwhelmed. How do I deal?

That makes sense. I hear you! Seeing 18 Modern Love Languages in front of you when you're used to just five can feel like a lot at first. The 18 in this book aren't meant to be memorized or categorized; they're more of a tool for exploration and self-reflection. Any overwhelm you're feeling will probably fade as you get more familiar with them and how they do or don't apply to your life!

How will I know which Languages for Modern Love are me?

Well, that's the thing — I don't believe that we "are" one (or more) love language. The ways we express love might be totally different from the ways we receive it AND our love languages may be different depending on the relationship. There's a good chance that multiple love languages in this book will — and won't! — resonate for different reasons and in different contexts, and that's kinda the point! All expressions of love are valid.

Is there a "right" way to read this book?

Nope! I recommend reading it through with no expectations or goals aside from seeing how you feel. Maybe keep paper or a notebook nearby in case something you read REALLY resonates so you can look back on it. (Or use the blank notes pages at the end of this book!) But, really, there are no rules here.

Is there a "wrong" way to read this book?

Well, right/wrong is binary talk and I'm not a fan, but it IS possible to use or experience this book in a way that's not intended and could feel icky.

Speaking from the Heart: 18 Languages for Modern Love is not an instruction manual or a tool to use to evaluate other people's abilities or assume their modern love languages. It's meant to help us recognize OUR needs and expressions of love and see what we feel capable of or comfortable with.

It's also not a checklist to make sure that you or someone else is "doing it right." The examples I give for each of the 18 Modern Love Languages are what they CAN look like, not what they MUST or SHOULD look like. The descriptions and their associated illustrations are meant to help us visualize or imagine what each Language for Modern Love could look or feel like, both on the giving and receiving end.

There is no expectation for folks to successfully enact each example of what the 18 Modern Love Languages can look like, (that would be ableist!), nor is there an expectation for people to resonate or be able to engage with all 18. The examples are there to help you better understand the 18 Modern Love Languages themselves and figure out what might feel good, what might feel missing, what might feel challenging, and what's outright on your "nope" list.

For example, I was recently diagnosed with ADHD. My brain and the way it expresses and processes thoughts and feelings has always been beautifully different. One of the 18 Modern Love Languages that I struggle with deeply is Platonic Touch, both on the giving and receiving end (but especially the giving). However, knowing that it's a powerful love language for others doesn't mean that I am lacking, less lovable, or "bad" at love. It also doesn't mean that the presence of Platonic Touch in the pages of this book somehow invalidates my experiences, my mind, or myself as a person. It simply means that Platonic Touch isn't a language I comfortably "speak" at this point in my life — though that could change in the future. Fortunately, Platonic Touch isn't my only option! Let's meet ourselves and others where we/they are at, not where they "should" be. Also, "should" statements are harmful!

Why is *Speaking from the Heart: 18 Languages for Modern Love* so heavily illustrated?

A few reasons:

- I genuinely don't believe we need another tome meant to tell us how to succeed in love and relationships.

- I don't believe that in order to effectively communicate information, it needs to be in longform. It might be what we're used to, but it's not the only way to educate.

- This book is meant to be accessible, inviting, welcoming, and "easy" to digest. Illustrations help with that.

- Not everyone learns or reads the same way, so why not have text AND images?

- I used illustrations to complement the written descriptions and I think it turned out great!

- The written word can only go so far. Visuals can help make concepts feel easier to understand.

- Illustrations are fun, and I like them.

Is there a quiz I can take?

Nope! The 18 Modern Love Languages aren't really "quizzable," but even if it was, I wouldn't make one! Hear me out:

In my experience using the love language concept with clients, I've found that *The 5 Love Languages*® quiz became people's main focal point. Viewers could simply answer 20-ish multiple choice questions and have their love language(s) presented to them in less than a minute. This took the introspection, critical thinking, consideration, and personal work out of the process, AND it sort of gave unspoken permission for folks to ignore or deprioritize the love languages that didn't show up in their quiz results, as if they didn't matter or apply to them.

It also turned the concept of love languages into a kind of personality test that people not only use to instantly qualify or disqualify romantic partners, but also make powerful value judgments on themselves and others.

Instead of a quiz, I created a workbook called *The Speaking from the Heart Workbook: A Practical Guide to the 18 Modern Love Languages* to help folks navigate the 18 Modern Love Languages and get clear about which ones they resonate with the most. It can be used solo OR with a partner and will NOT gamify the process or categorize you!

My hope is that you read through the 18 Modern Love Languages in this book with no goal other than being open and maybe even curious. Notice what resonates and what doesn't. Explore how each one might look and feel in the various relationships in your life AND if they'd resonate differently if you were on the receiving end vs. giving end. Notice which of the 18 Modern Love Languages feel significant to you but also intimidating or challenging.

Whatever comes up for you while reading is valid and true for you and only you — please let go of any judgments! — and will provide powerful pieces of information that you can use as you navigate your inner and outer world.

Alrighty! Now that we've got that squared away, let's start looking at some updated and expansive ways that humans give, receive, and identify love.

THE 18 MODERN LOVE LANGUAGES

1. ACCOUNTABILITY — 35

2. ACTIVE LISTENING — 38

3. ACTS OF EMPATHY — 41

4. AFFIRMING COMMUNICATION — 44

5. BESTOWING — 47

6. EMOTIONAL LABOR — 50

7. ENGAGED EXPERIENCES — 53

8. INTENTIONAL TIME — 56

9. PERSONAL GROWTH — 59

THE 18 MODERN LOVE LANGUAGES

10. PLATONIC TOUCH	**62**
11. PROBLEM-SOLVING	**65**
12. PROVIDING	**68**
13. SHARED BELIEFS	**71**
14. SOLIDARITY	**74**
15. TEAMWORK	**77**
16. THOUGHTFUL SERVICE	**80**
17. UNDIVIDED ATTENTION	**83**
18. UPSKILLING	**86**

#1 ACCOUNTABILITY

Mistakes and conflict are a part of being human AND being in relationship, which means Accountability is a valuable skill to cultivate and practice for most of us. It isn't always easy to acknowledge our part in a conflict or miscommunication, recognize the harm we've caused, and respond to a loved one's hurt feelings with empathy and an apology; however, these are important social skills that can lead to resolution. There's more than one way to take Accountability and apologize, so don't be surprised if a simple "I'm sorry" doesn't cut the mustard.

#1 ACCOUNTABILITY CAN LOOK LIKE:

- Accepting responsibility for actions
- An unsolicited apology
- Following through on changes
- A sincere apology
- "How can I make this right, if I can?"
- "I" statements
- Acknowledging impact
- Feeling uncomfortable

#1 ACCOUNTABILITY IS <u>NOT</u>:

"I'm sorry, OK?"

Begging for forgiveness

Focusing on your intent

Making promises or commitments you can't keep

Making a "both sides" argument

A blame game

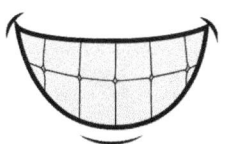
Making sure everyone is happy

Saying "the right thing"

#2 ACTIVE LISTENING

Active Listening is especially important for those of us who need to feel heard in order to feel loved. This involves intentional body language and some key communication tools — such as leaning in, asking clarifying questions, and paraphrasing — and being truly present with your loved one. It means participating in the conversation with intention and attention while giving them the floor, and any opinions or judgments about what they've shared are best kept to yourself (unless they're solicited!).

#2 ACTIVE LISTENING CAN LOOK LIKE:

"Wow, what happened next?"

An open, curious mind

"Did I get that right?"

Exploratory questions

"I heard you say..."

Leaning in

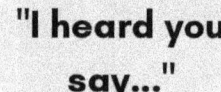

Eye contact

Nodding your head

#2 ACTIVE LISTENING IS NOT:

Peeking at your phone

Closed-ended questions

Avoiding eye contact

"I don't get it."

Pretending to be interested

"Hm, cool."

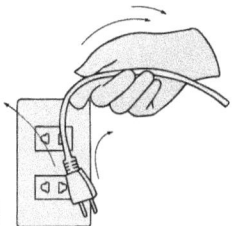
Changing the subject

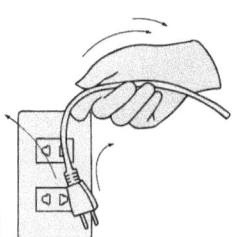
Disengaging

#3 ACTS OF EMPATHY

So many of us want to feel understood and Acts of Empathy can be a powerful tool for getting there. Putting ourselves in others' shoes and seeing their perspective can help us relate to lived experiences that aren't our own — an important part of community-building — and being on the receiving end of that effort can feel amazing. Remember: empathy is not synonymous with understanding. You don't have to 100% understand someone to respect them and their feelings.

#3 ACTS OF EMPATHY CAN LOOK LIKE:

 Listening quietly

Asking for their perspective

"Do you want advice or to just feel heard?"

"How can I support you?"

"How does that make you feel?"

 Acknowledging and validating their pain

"That sounds hard."

Putting yourself in their shoes

#3 ACTS OF EMPATHY ARE NOT:

 **Waiting to share your point of view**

Toxic positivity

"I don't believe you."

Minimizing, questioning, or invalidating pain

Unsolicited advice

 **Empty platitudes**

"Just don't let it bother you."

Playing devil's advocate

#4 AFFIRMING COMMUNICATION

Hearing or reading words that commend or acknowledge us can light up our brain's reward center and help us receive compliments and admiration that might feel out of reach in our own minds. Affirming Communication isn't just about praising physical features; this is a powerful way to help someone feel seen, heard, and valued for who they are — not just what they look like. There are many different ways to communicate our affection, awe, respect, and love for someone, so get creative!

#4 AFFIRMING COMMUNICATION CAN LOOK LIKE:

Praise for efforts, accomplishments, and little victories

"I believe in you."

"I'm proud of you."

 Memes, texts, gifs, & emails

 Supportive words during challenges

 "Those shoes are AMAZING."

Writing & sharing Gratitude Lists

Post-its on the mirror

#4 AFFIRMING COMMUNICATION IS <u>NOT</u>:

Obligatory compliments

Centering beauty standards

 "Thanks, you too."

Self-aggrandizing

 An item on your to-do list

Ego stroking

A replacement for Acts of Empathy

 Something to expect or require from others

#5 BESTOWING

Feeling love through giving or receiving gifts gets a lot of flack, as it's often associated with superficiality, a substitute for other expressions of love, or a distraction from (or apology for) not meeting someone's actual relationship needs. But that's not what Bestowing or gift-giving as a love language is about! Giving and receiving gifts is a tangible representation of exchange, which can have a powerful impact on relationships of all kinds. Remember: Bestowing isn't just pricey purchases and shiny wrapping — though they're 100% valid! — so, if you notice yourself feeling a little judgy about this one, take a breath and keep reading.

#5 BESTOWING CAN LOOK LIKE:

Something given without expectation of reciprocity

Something handmade

Special occasion gifts, like breakfast in bed

Gifting time or energy

Material gifts (something with a price tag)

Unexpected surprises, like pulling over to watch the sunset

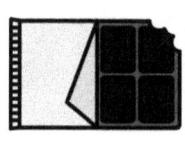
Thinking-of-you gifts, like their fave candy

Sharing knowledge

#5 BESTOWING IS NOT:

A substitute for emotional connection

A test or proof of love or commitment

A way to get what you want

Hinting what they should give you

Inherently expensive: high price tag stronger love

Currency (no one owes a gift)

An apology replacement

Shallow, meaningless, or "buying love"

#6 EMOTIONAL LABOR

Emotional Labor is a culturally undervalued and under-respected work form, typically performed by women and folks who were socialized with feminine gender roles. And, while Emotional Labor doesn't come with a paycheck, it's an incredibly valuable — priceless, even — expression of care, love, and respect. People of all genders can benefit from Emotional Labor — on both the giving and receiving end. Some forms of Emotional Labor are small, hard to measure, and even invisible. So, be patient if you're still learning how to notice and take some of this on (and off your loved one's shoulders). Don't forget the power of voicing gratitude in return.

#6 EMOTIONAL LABOR CAN LOOK LIKE:

 **Planning and taking the lead**

Remembering important names and dates

 **Initiating important conversations**

 **Managing your emotions in challenging situations**

Being an outlet for unprocessed emotions

 **Making choices and decisions**

Anticipating needs

"I'll handle it."

#6 EMOTIONAL LABOR IS <u>NOT</u>:

 Easily measurable, tangible actions

"Women's work"

 Avoidant behaviors

 Grand gestures

Something that "just comes naturally."

 Skills you'd find on a resume

 Something men aren't good at.

 Free therapy (or a therapy replacement)

#7 ENGAGED EXPERIENCES

Doing something you want to do with someone you care about can have powerful effects on your sense of connection and belonging — and, depending on the activity or experience, you may also end up building an even stronger sense of trust and ease. For some, this might look like taking an adventurous vacation in the woods while, for others, Engaged Experiences look more like waiting to watch that new cat video until you're together and can get that dopamine hit at the same time.

#7 ENGAGED EXPERIENCES CAN LOOK LIKE:

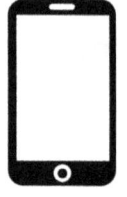 **DMing each other memes**

 **Watching each other's fave shows**

 **Trying something new & unfamiliar**

Exploring new places

Participating in activism

 **Visiting family**

Listening to elders share stories

 **Joining a live stream**

#7 ENGAGED EXPERIENCES ARE NOT:

Just about risk-taking & adrenaline rushes

A substitute for Intentional Time

An excuse to go on vacation

A way to get them to finally watch that Sci-fi series

Only engaging to you

A substitute for communication

Inherently expensive

Distractions from conflict

#8 INTENTIONAL TIME

The concept of time can be tricky; on one hand, it can feel like we have all the time in the world while, on the other, time seems to fly by so quickly that February turns into June in the blink of an eye. This is why prioritizing uninterrupted time with those you love can play a major role in maintaining the connection and bond that drew you together in the first place. It communicates how much you value them, their time, and their energy. Intentional Time is often an important one for folks in romantic and sexual relationships, but it's not exclusively so. Friendships and families require opportunities for folks to be together with no motive other than enjoying each other's company, too. And the best part? Intentional Time doesn't have to cost a dime.

#8 INTENTIONAL TIME CAN LOOK LIKE:

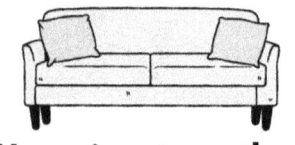 **Napping together on the couch**

 **Deliberately scheduling it**

Prioritizing important conversations

 **Turning off phones & devices**

One-on-one hangouts/dates

Parallel play

Co-working

Doing nothing together

#8 INTENTIONAL TIME IS <u>NOT</u>:

 **Tagging along on a business trip**

 **Deprioritizing other responsibilities**

Quantity (lots of time quality)

 **Piggybacking on someone else's time**

Constant disruptions

Centering your schedule only

 **Fitting someone in**

 **Simply being in the same room**

#9 PERSONAL GROWTH

This is a particularly significant one. Humans are complicated and ever-evolving. That means that in order to grow we have to acknowledge our limitations and pledge to some form of individual healing or development as we get older, and learn more about ourselves and the world. Whether through consistent therapy, maintaining a spiritual practice, or seeking support from others (and paying for it), a commitment to Personal Growth recognizes that the relationship we have with ourselves is the most important relationship we have - a language of love directed toward ourselves! Personal Growth benefits us AND the relationships we are in — even if it means we outgrow some of them as we do it.

#9 PERSONAL GROWTH CAN LOOK LIKE:

 Trauma therapy

 Setting & respecting boundaries

 Ending relationships that no longer serve you

 Trying out different coping skills

 Talking about how you feel

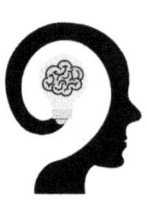 Unlearning harmful belief systems

 Interdependence

 Being curious instead of accusatory

#9 PERSONAL GROWTH IS <u>NOT</u>:

Performative

Staying comfortable

Expecting others to grow with you or the same way

A superficial gesture

Getting bangs or a makeover

Proof you're a good person

"Good vibes only"

A way to absolve you from harm you've caused

 PLATONIC TOUCH

Platonic Touch encompasses any kind of physical contact without sexual intent — in other words, expressing connection and affection vs. expressing sexual desire. This kind of contact can evoke chemical responses in the brain that assist in bonding, but it also carries important conditions. Effectively communicating Platonic Touch requires awareness of others' personal space and comfort levels, especially when they're different from yours (another way to express care and respect!). For those on the receiving end of Platonic Touch, setting limits and boundaries is not rude or a rejection; it's an important (and often misunderstood) expression of respect that lets others know what kind of physical touch feels OK. Also, if other humans aren't around, we can replicate some of these comforting Platonic Touch sensations with non-human options!

#10 PLATONIC TOUCH CAN LOOK LIKE:

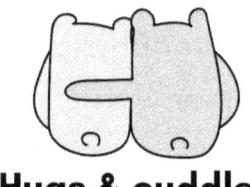
Hugs & cuddles

Head resting on a shoulder

Weighted blankets

"May I hold your hand?"

Snuggling with a pet

Using an exfoliator, body oil, lotion, or skin cream that feels special

Somatic self-touch

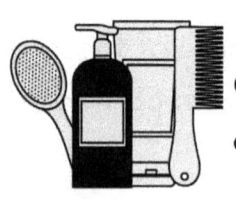
Grooming each other

#10 PLATONIC TOUCH IS <u>NOT</u>:

A way to measure love

Permission to touch everyone

Something everyone wants

Touching others on your terms

Sexual touch

Foreplay or initiating sex

An obligation or requirement

A way to tell how "healed" or "healthy" someone is

#11 PROBLEM-SOLVING

Sometimes we don't just want to be heard, we really need help figuring something out. Problem-Solving can be a meaningful expression of love when we're feeling overwhelmed, alone, and unsure of what to do — as long as it's clear we're looking for solutions. When we're the ones offering possible solutions, it's important to manage our expectations about the outcome and be prepared for our suggestions to be rejected (it happens). Taking on some responsibility through Problem-Solving can be a particularly impactful expression of love and support to a friend or significant other, especially during times of deep distress and grief.

#11 PROBLEM-SOLVING CAN LOOK LIKE:

 Researching & notetaking

 Doing what needs to be done without being asked

 Trouble-shooting

 Being a sounding board

 "I'll handle this."

 Making or managing phone calls

 Having a backup plan just in case

 Solicited advice

#11 PROBLEM-SOLVING IS <u>NOT</u>:

 **Telling someone what to do**

 **Steamrolling whoever is in charge**

 **Trying to change or control how someone feels**

 **Unsolicited advice, help, or suggestions**

 **Patronizing or condescending instructions**

 **Proving you were right or know better**

 **Having all the answers**

 **A competition you must win**

#12 PROVIDING

Being a provider comes in many forms and is not limited to the financial, and this form of caregiving isn't exclusively a maternal or household act (though it certainly can be!). However Providing presents itself, caring for the needs and safety of someone can be a powerful expression of love, but ONLY when all parties involved consent to that dynamic. This is not to be conflated with the socially constructed gender-based roles of Provider and Caregiver, heteronormative tropes that have historically been used to excuse systemic harm and oppression. Providing gives us an opportunity to home in on how we genuinely feel about giving or receiving caregiving free from outside (or internalized) judgement, and if we might benefit from reframing these actions to better suit our own experience.

#12 PROVIDING CAN LOOK LIKE:

Supplying housing or shelter

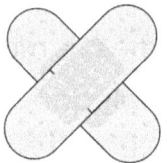
Giving care during an illness

Sharing food, supplies, tools, and more

Charitable support, donations, and sponsorships

Homemaking

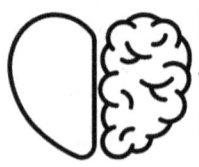
Passing down wisdom and knowledge

Caring for other people's children

Sugarmamas, Sugardaddies, Glucose Guardians & Sugarbabies

#12 PROVIDING IS <u>NOT</u>:

 An excuse to avoid accountability

 A way to establish control

"Men's work"

 An obligation, requirement, or expectation

 Infantilization

 Enforcement of gender roles

 Having or giving lots of money

 Parenting

#13 SHARED BELIEFS

If Teamwork (#15) is the glue, Shared Beliefs are the foundation that relationships are built on. Having the same core beliefs — belief systems that are integral and foundational for each of you — establishes a sense of trust, belonging, and safety that can be a powerful way to maintain a connection. We don't often spend intentional time communicating about our beliefs with loved ones, in part because we might not be 100% sure of what they are, but getting clear on what matters most and seeing where our beliefs overlap can provide a potent sense of safety and understanding. Plus, knowing what we can live with (night person vs. morning person or mismatched food tastes) and our dealbreakers (maybe religious beliefs or political leanings) can be a fast and effective way to evaluate compatibility and save ourselves some time and emotion.

#13 SHARED BELIEFS CAN LOOK LIKE:

Political leanings

Common religion

Favorite bands or movies

Drug or alcohol use

Life roles and responsibilities

Common values

Preferred relationship styles

Laughing at the same jokes

#13 SHARED BELIEFS ARE NOT:

Liking all the same things

A substitute for shared core values

Criticizing or judging others

An excuse for bigotry, hate, or harm

Agreeing on EVERYTHING

A way to coerce someone into joining a group

Guaranteed safety or compatibility

Never fighting or arguing

#14 SOLIDARITY

Showing Solidarity is the emotional equivalent of playing on the same team and knowing that someone's got your back. There's a sense of ease and community that comes from this and it can show up on almost any scale — from individual friendships to international social media campaigns. One of the best parts of Solidarity is that we can do it for almost anyone — we don't even need to know the person's name. In cultures that have systemic oppression baked into their foundations, exhibiting Solidarity toward our fellow humans is important and, dare we say, essential for the wellbeing of future generations. Whether by putting one's comfort or body on the line, speaking up to those in power, believing survivors, calling out jokes that punch down, or something else entirely, Solidarity can be a deeply impactful and healing expression of love and respect.

#14 SOLIDARITY CAN LOOK LIKE:

Trusting and believing others' experiences

Prioritizing others' humanity over your comfort

Standing up for people (including strangers)

Showing support when it doesn't benefit you

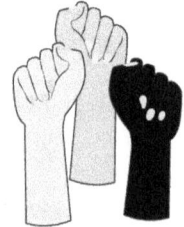

Calling out/in/on harmful behavior

Standing on the frontlines at protests and rallies

Stepping back to make space for others

"Are you OK?"

#14 SOLIDARITY IS <u>NOT</u>:

- Proof that you're "one of the good ones"
-  "Just asking questions"
- Defending someone simply because they're your friend
- Aligning with harmful viewpoints
-  A way to collect rewards or "cookies"
-  Weaponizing your privilege or power
- A byproduct of marriage
- Permanent loyalty

#15 TEAMWORK

Something powerful happens when two or more people work together on something that requires cooperation, skill-sharing, and collaboration. For some, Teamwork can be the glue that keeps bonds strong and helps shift an adversarial "us vs. them" mindset into a more compassionate "you + me" headspace. Initiating this shift is a powerful expression of love. Teamwork is especially useful for folks who find it easy to emotionally disconnect from their partners — few things reconnect us quicker than remembering what makes us such a good team.

#15 TEAMWORK CAN LOOK LIKE:

 Cooperative activities like escape rooms, tandem bikes, and RPGs

 Working together to find solutions

 Doing a puzzle

 Sharing household and/or childcare responsibilities

Starting or running a business together

 Asking for and receiving help

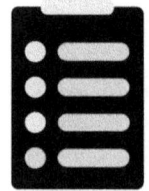 Diving and delegating tasks equitably

 Working out conflicts collaboratively

#15 TEAMWORK IS NOT:

Giving orders

A strategy for avoiding your own responsibilities

Non-consensual power play

Convincing others to follow your lead

Co-dependence

Making demands

Winning vs. losing

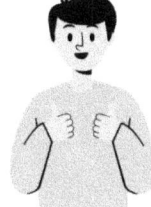
Everyone agreeing with each other

#16 THOUGHTFUL SERVICE

Participating in our communities (local or global) can help us feel connected to something outside of ourselves and make an immediate impact on those around us, regardless of whether you're face to face or continents apart. This type of service can also give us a sense of purpose in a world that, for many of us, can feel overwhelming and leave us uncertain about our place. The key here is to do something for someone without expectation of them doing the same for us, or anything in return, and without them needing to ask or do something to deserve it. The intention is service, not reciprocity, and managing our expectations is key.

#16 THOUGHTFUL SERVICE CAN LOOK LIKE:

Handling chores that aren't typically yours

Donations or volunteer work

Offering referrals

Holding the door for a stranger

Making or prepping meals

Giving up your chair

Walking your friend to their car, home, or the subway

Being a friend's emergency contact

#16 THOUGHTFUL SERVICE IS NOT:

 Proof you're a good person

 Doing something only when asked

 Tit-for-tat scorekeeping

A substitute for Affirming Communication

 Assuming someone needs your help because of their age, ability, gender, etc.

 "Women's work"

 Something you do to get something in return

Assuming strangers will want your help

#17 UNDIVIDED ATTENTION

Few things can leave someone feeling more seen and heard than Undivided Attention. This means that whatever you might be doing together — Intentional Time, Engaged Experiences, Providing — you're not sharing or splitting your attention with someone or something else. Doing so allows others to feel important, prioritized, and valued and shows how much you WANT to see them, hear from them, or share something. While many of us are overworked and overextended, finding opportunities to focus on the people you love (and only the people you love) can feel incredibly nourishing for everyone involved.

#17 UNDIVIDED ATTENTION CAN LOOK LIKE:

 **No phones, TVs, or devices**

 **Eye contact**

 **A quiet environment**

 **One-on-one or small groups**

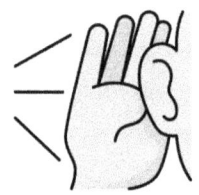 **Active Listening**

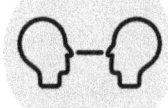 **Attentive body language**

 **Blocking off or reserving time**

 **Prioritizing the person over any interruptions**

#17 UNDIVIDED ATTENTION IS <u>NOT</u>:

Watching sports in the background

Multitasking

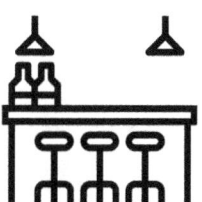
Hanging out at a crowded bar

Group dates

Pretending to be interested because it's "polite"

Daydreaming

Checking your phone every time it beeps

Planning your day while they talk

#18 UPSKILLING

Learning from each other can be a powerful bonding tool and keeps relationships interesting! We get to give each other a platform to talk and teach about something important, and sometimes we end up learning something brand new about the subject — and our loved one. Having that communication is a way to Upskill for each other. Being in an educator role can feel empowering and energizing; receiving new information from someone we care about can be inspiring and ignite a sense of curiosity and creativity that can nourish a relationship. Upskilling sparks interest in each other and a desire to continue to learn from and about the people in our lives.

#18 UPSKILLING CAN LOOK LIKE:

Receiving with gratitude

"Can you help me understand this?"

Taking a class or course together

Sharing stories

"Will you tell me more about that?"

"Would you like me to show you?"

 **Asking exploratory questions**

 **Sharing how-to videos**

#18 UPSKILLING IS <u>NOT</u>:

Lecturing or soapboxing

Asking yes or no questions

Unsolicited information

Condescending or patronizing

A test of intelligence

Just doing it for them

Weaponized incompetence

Something to feel embarrassed or insecure about

YOU MADE IT THROUGH!

LET'S DO A CHECK-IN:

- ♡ HOW DO YOU FEEL?

- ♡ DID ANY STAND OUT TO YOU?

- ♡ DID YOU RECOGNIZE ANY LOVED ONES AS YOU READ?

- ♡ DID ANY LEAVE YOU FEELING A LITTLE ACTIVATED?

SPEAKING OF ACTIVATED...
(KEEP READING)

A NOTE ABOUT SELF- & CO-REGULATION:

When we get activated, experience conflict, or find ourselves feeling uncomfortable, anxious, or disconnected, learning to self-regulate or co-regulate (depending on our situation) can be incredibly helpful. The 18 Modern Love Languages in this book may be a useful tool for exploring and identifying the actions, sounds, words, and sensations that help you through these experiences.

(Remember: no matter your relationship status, you're in a relationship with yourself 24/7, so you can use many of these 18 Modern Love Languages to show yourself some care.)

Self-regulation is a process that often involves forms of self-soothing, self-exploration, physical movement, meditation, breathwork, and other body-centered or mindfulness practices. The goal here is to support yourself as you shift from a reactive place into a more grounded and centered place. As the name suggests, this is done on your own.

Co-regulation is a similar process, but instead of rolling solo, you and your loved one intentionally engage in soothing, connecting, and affirming activities together. The goal is to support each other and shift from a disconnected or adversarial headspace using the 18 Modern Love Languages with which you most resonate. That might look like alternating between tools and activities that help you and ones that help your loved one. Affirming Communication might be a great place to start.

Please keep this in mind: it's not our responsibility to soothe our partners or loved ones, nor should we manage their emotional states (that's their job!). But if we'd like to show support during dysregulated times, we can use one or more of these 18 Modern Love Languages to do it. Just make sure to avoid prioritizing your loved one's needs over your own, as it can fuel resentment and leave you feeling unsupported.

Think of it like the oxygen mask analogy: when you're on an airplane, attendants specifically instruct you to put on your own mask before helping others put on theirs. It might sound a little backwards at first, and by no means am I comparing relationship challenges to airplane emergencies, but one of the most powerful expressions of love, care, and respect for others is prioritizing your own mental and emotional wellbeing. Doing so helps you show up for yourself and your loved ones to the best of your ability, and when (not if) conflict and triggers do happen, you have tools to help you navigate through them — on your own AND together.

A PERSONAL THANK-YOU TO MY FAVORITE CO-REGULATORS:

HARRIET & BURT

SOME POINTS TO REMEMBER:

Before you go, I wanted to leave you with some important takeaways about 18 Modern Love Languages and how to incorporate them into your life (if you want to).

First: Don't forget that 18 Modern Love Languages and love languages in general are an anecdotal idea, NOT a psychological or scientific study. That doesn't mean they don't have value, of course, but it does mean that they must be thought about, shared, and used with care and thought.

These are socially constructed ideas about expressing and exchanging love based on observations, considerations, and personal relational experiences, which means that they may not apply to all people in the same way (or at all) and they cannot responsibly be used as some kind of universal measurement tool of a person's value, worth, or compatibility as a friend, roommate, romantic or sexual partner, or something else.

Please don't lump yourself or others into categories based on the 18 Modern Love Languages that they do or don't resonate with.

Like all experiences with emotion, how we express and receive love will fluctuate and be different day to day, relationship to relationship. Love languages are fluid and need space to move, shift, grow, change, and expand as you do. Make space for them to look, feel, and sound differently from person to person. Please don't treat them like a health diagnosis, personality trait, or tattoo.

Second: Consider the 18 Modern Love Languages as a tool among the many other tools that exist for navigating your relationship to yourself and others. It is not the end all be all, nor the single exclusive concept that can solve your relational challenges and lead you to your true loves.

Make the ideas in this book and the 18 Modern Love Languages work for you and your relationships. There are no "rules" and there is no "right" way to have a connection with someone. Every person you meet is going to require something different from you and you're likely going to require something different from them in return – because none of us feel, think, look, or behave exactly the same and we often don't know what we need in a relationship until we notice that something feels like it's missing.

If rules help you feel grounded and in control, then make your own rules for yourself to follow. If you're in a relationship of some kind, then collaborate on a set of rules that make sense and feel right to everyone involved. And be willing and prepared to adjust, edit, or throw them away at any moment.

Third: After reading this book and as you go about your days, you might recognize more than 18 Modern Love Languages, that you or someone else does or says strikes you in a way that you can feel in your body. That's AMAZING. Write them down! Use them! Add them to the notes pages in the back of this book!

You are the expert of yourself, your experiences, and if or how the 18 Modern Love Languages show up in your life. Don't let anyone tell you otherwise. But at the same time, keep in mind that everyone else in your life is the expert of themselves, their experiences, and if or how the 18 Modern Love Languages show up for them. Make space for a variety of perspectives and interpretations of these concepts, including ones that to you feel completely wrong or ridiculous. Despite what we're often told, we don't know better than other people and we don't want to venture into territory that veers on the edge of patronizing, controlling, or superior.

Fourth: As you try out the 18 Modern Love Languages in your relationships, keep in mind that the impact of your actions matters more than your intent. Something might not land the way you thought it would, not because you did something wrong but because humans can be unpredictable with murky or inconsistent feelings and we can't read other people's minds. Don't be surprised if something doesn't work or feel good to you or the people you're in relationship with – it's kinda just part of the deal with choosing to engage and interact with other humans!

I would venture to guess that a majority of the time, you have nothing but kind or positive intentions behind the things you do and say, so your intent isn't in question! The clincher is that sometimes we act in a way that makes complete sense to us, or even in a way that we wish others would to us, but it ends up landing wonkily and upsetting someone. Regardless of how well-intended we were, we ended up hurting or harming someone by accident and now we have to decide how we want to handle it.

Taking responsibility for our actions (Accountability!) can be a powerful expression of love and respect for someone – including complete strangers you may never see again – and it doesn't have to be a big show. In fact, most of the time, what is needed is some kind of acknowledgment, maybe an apology, and then moving the heck on. Making a big deal out of it, begging for forgiveness, or showing repentance often ends up making the situation more about you and your feelings (especially your fear of being judged or punished) and doesn't address the person you harmed. And it can make the situation worse than it was before you attempted to take responsibility!

Sometimes, the most effective response in the moment sounds something like, "I'm sorry, thank you for telling me." At times when you don't feel sorry at all, maybe even attacked or irritated, please don't pretend. Try saying something like, "Thanks for letting me know. Let me get back to you once I have a moment to let this sink in." The gratitude isn't for having been called out or corrected in some way – it's gratitude for the person who chose to say something instead of pretending everything was fine and made space for the opportunity to deal with it and move on without friction, resentment, or passive aggressive b.s. It may sting or zing in the moment, and that's OK. Wait for the sting or zing to subside or go away completely before saying what needs to be said.

WANT TO KEEP EXPLORING?

Dive deeper into your relationship to love with *The Speaking from the Heart Workbook: A Practical Guide to the Languages for Modern Love.*

It's available in digital AND print form!

ANNE HODDER-SHIPP, CSE

THE SPEAKING FROM THE HEART WORKBOOK

A PRACTICAL GUIDE TO THE 18 MODERN LOVE LANGUAGES

50+ EXERCISES & WORKSHEETS INSIDE!

FOLLOW ANNE ONLINE!

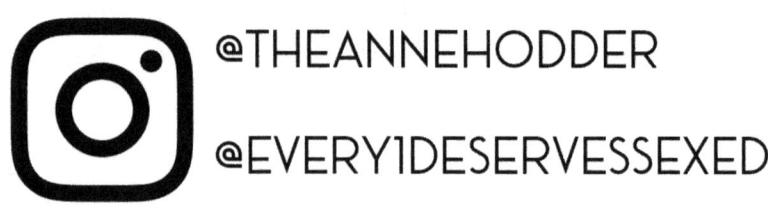 @THEANNEHODDER
@EVERY1DESERVESSEXED

 @THEANNEHODDER

ABOUT THE AUTHOR:

Image description: Anne is wearing a mint green blazer and white tank top, and she is smiling big at the camera. Her hair is short, with one side a little longer than the other, and blond, and she is wearing big gold glasses.

Anne Hodder-Shipp (she/they) is an AASECT Award-winning certified sex and relationships educator and dreamwork practitioner who's worked in the field of sexuality since 2007. Their candid commentary and informed perspective about sex, identity, and relationships have appeared in Glamour; O, The Oprah Magazine; Men's Health; Teen Vogue; The Washington Post; and more.

Anne lives with her spouse, Nathaniel, and their five cats: Harriet, Luci, George, Beatrice, and Lester.

LOOKING FOR PROFESSIONAL & PERSONAL DEVELOPMENT LIKE THIS?

If you enjoyed or felt inspired by this, you might enjoy my other heart-centered offerings! Check them out:

Compassionate sex & relationship coaching, private sex education for teens & tweens, plus dreamwork.
www.annehoddershipp.com

Empowered sex education classes & events, plus professional development trainings & certification.
www.everyonedeservessexed.com

Live & recorded courses that help you find more pleasure & joy.
www.s3xplus.com

WANT TO WORK WITH ME?

15%
DISCOUNT

This coupon can be used to book a private virtual coaching, dreamwork, or professional development session with Anne.

https://bit.ly/hireanne

Use code: MLLWORKBOOK

CHEERS!

Image description: Anne is wearing a white button-up collared shirt with long sleeves, and she is smiling at the camera while holding a pretty-looking cocktail in a vintage stemmed glass. Her hair is shoulder-length and blond, and she is wearing her usual big gold glasses. Her armadillo tattoo (her name is Helen) on her forearm is peeking out from under her sleeve.

NOTES

NOTES

NOTES

NOTES

NOTES

www.ingramcontent.com/pod-product-compliance
Lightning Source LLC
Chambersburg PA
CBHW071714020426
42333CB00017B/2263